THE LIFE AND WORK OF ROBERT WATTS

Dr R E L Rodgers

Christian Focus Publications

Published by
Christian Focus Publications Ltd.

Tain   Houston
Ross-shire   Texas

© 1989 DR R E L RODGERS

ISBN 1 871676 15 0

Christian Focus Publications is a non-denominational publishing house. The views expressed are those of the authors.

For Eric and Letty Lawley

Foreword by

Very Rev. John T Carson BA DD

As secretary of the Presbyterian Historical Society of Ireland, at one of whose meetings Dr Rodgers delivered the gist of this book as a lecture, I have the greatest pleasure in commending it to all who love the Reformed faith, to preachers and pastors, and to their people as well. May it be used to deepen interest in this noble system and bring glory to God.

Theology was once called the 'Queen of sciences' and when she ruled there was a general peace in the Church, in its worship, and in Christian experience. Unfortunately that does not pertain to the present time; ephemeral tastes and a shallow sentimentality have taken over in many quarters. This timely little volume about the Rev. Prof. Robert Watts, an Ulster-Scot American who became Professor of Systematic Theology at Assembly's College, Belfast in 1866, arrives on a scene over which theology enjoys only a limited monarchy.

Robert Watts was one of a vast number of Ulster lads who left their homeland for the New World in the nineteenth century. He had been a teacher of sorts in Ireland but in America he found the opportunity to develop and increase his many God-given faculties. He arrived at Princeton Theological Seminary in 1847, via Lafayette College. This was the Princeton of Charles Hodge and J. Addison Alexander, and Watts found it fertile soil for the roots of his love for the Reformed faith, as it is found in the Westminster standards, its Confession of Faith and its two famous Catechisms.

After a few years in a congregation in Philadelphia he was compelled to return to Ireland because of his wife's health and the outbreak of the Civil War. He was almost immediately called by the Presbyterian congregation in Lower Gloucester St. in Dublin. Only a few years later a vacancy arose in the Belfast college, and Watts was unanimously appointed to a Chair which attracted an unprecedented number of students from Scotland.

From the beginning he was an exact, and some thought an exacting, theologian, but theologian he most certainly was. To him the Bible's authority was indisputable and doctrine mattered a great deal. The doctrine of God both in nature and in grace was at the very centre of all his thinking and the supreme motivation of his entire life. For Robert Watts this was no straitjacket awkward and irksome. He gloried in the sense of duty which his faith imposed upon him and he rejoiced in the freedom which he felt in the service of his Sovereign Lord.

It is permissible to ask here, 'Why resurrect an old Victorian theologian now? What relevance can he have today?' The first reason that I can think about is that we need to be reminded nowadays that the person and work of God in Christ should be the supreme subject of preaching, and no one can say that today's preaching is overloaded with theology.

Another thing Watts will remind us about is that the Christian minister is called to be a Mr Standfast as well as an Evangelist, a Mr Valiant-for-the-Truth as well as a Mr Greatheart. Both his friends and those who disagreed with him were united in one thing, namely, that 'he waged an unceasing warfare in his lectures and in his writings and in the Press'. He considered that such a solid defence of the orthodox faith was no more than he had promised at his ordination. Of course it is a difficult thing to do well, convincingly and without rancour, and there are some who claim to be evangelical but who are not set for the defence of the Gospel and who need to be reminded of this obligation.

Furthermore, there are far too many Christians today who think that theology is old style and out of fashion; indeed as far as Christian witness and living are concerned they think it is really possible to dispense with it altogether. Dr George Matheson once declared that Christians may mount up with wings but they must be wings of thought. Too much of today's religious activity, its writing and its worship is not marked as it should be with 'awe and wonder and with bated breath'. Watts' theology and his life bore these clear hallmarks, and it would be my wish that this brief but carefully written biography would contribute to their revival in the Church of today.

Room 217, Church House,
Fisherwick Place,
BELFAST. BT1 6DW

The life and work of Robert Watts

In one of the more prosperous farms in the district of Moneylane, Co Down, Robert Watts was born on the 10th July 1820, 311 years after John Calvin, whose birthdate he shared and whose teachings he was afterwards to propagate with such singular success.

Watts' father was a God-fearing Presbyterian farmer whose major concern was that his children should be taught the Scriptures and the Westminster Confession. This early teaching was particularly valuable to Robert, the youngest of the fourteen children in the Watts' family, and it imparted to him an exact knowledge of the Word of God and its doctrine which laid the foundations of the theological ability so characteristic of his later years.

Because of the deadness and cold formality of so many churches, those who were concerned for the preservation and maintenance of a truly biblical ministry were forced to convene services outside the confines of the churches altogether. Thus, Watts' father, a man of decided Christian character and cheerful temperament, opened his home to itinerant preachers of the Gospel. Robert's earliest recollections would therefore have been of a large family, housed in reasonably comfortable conditions, dispensing hospitality to all around and playing its part in spreading the Gospel of the Grace of God.

His mother was a woman of great ability and eminent piety who exerted upon her children a powerful influence for good. His father's death when Robert was only seven years of age dealt a heavy blow to the entire family and placed an onerous burden of responsibility upon the mother. She was equal to the task, however, and in later years Robert was accustomed to say that he owed a debt to his mother which could never fully be repaid.

Watts' introduction to education took place at the parish school at Kilmagan near to his home, and this, of course, was a school run by the Episcopal Church. Later, when he was at a more advanced stage of learning and the school was further from his home, his brothers would take it in turn to carry young Robert there on their shoulders.

During these formative years he acquired a love for education that he never relinquished and his first intentions were to become a schoolmaster. To this end, he studied for a time in Dublin and later taught school at Mountpanther. Eventually, however, he returned to Belfast to resume his studies at the Belfast Academical Institution.

Over the years the family began to split up as one and another sought to make his way in the world. Two brothers went to Philadelphia in America where they established a prosperous business. In 1847, it was decided that the other members of the family should join the two in America, and Robert, then twenty seven years of age, faced the prospect of life in the New World. This move involved leaving for a time the one who was later to become his devoted wife for more than forty years. She was Margaret, daughter of William Newell of Summer Hill, Downpatrick.

From the moment he arrived in America, Watts undertook further study. He went first of all to Lafayette College, Virginia, where he formed a life-long friendship with the family of the College President, the Reverend Dr George Junkin. Upon the removal to Washington College of President Junkin, Watts followed him there, and graduated in 1849 with the degree of Bachelor of Arts. This institution, which later became Washington and Lee University, was also to award Watts the degree of Doctor of Laws.

He proceeded next to Princeton in New Jersey. That Seminary was to have an abiding effect upon Watts and 'he never lost the impress given to his personal character and theological views at Princeton'. His diploma is dated 18 May 1852 and is signed by Charles Hodge, J Addison Alexander and W H Green. Among Watts' classmates at Princeton were Caspar Wistar Hodge Snr (son of Charles Hodge) and James Pettigrew Boyce - Principal Founder of the first Southern Baptist Seminary (in 1859).

The First Pastorate

Watts' pastoral work began in a missionary context. During his three years at Princeton he had impressed his professors with his spirituality and academic ability, and when his course had only three weeks to run he learned that he had been appointed by the Presbytery of Philadelphia for mission work at Moyamensing. This was a neglected area of Philadelphia and would offer the prospect of exceedingly difficult ministerial labour. In the work at Moyamensing Watts exhibited those qualities which were to characterise his ministry for the rest of his life - qualities of intense earnestness and application that would finally exhaust him, and wrest from him a life wholly dedicated to God.

Labouring under the difficulties usually associated with a Church Extension Charge, and with those trials peculiar to the area in which Providence had placed him, the young minister succeeded in drawing together a warmly attached congregation which met in those early years in Franklin House Hall. In due course a building was erected on Broad Street, Philadelphia, for the use of the congregation, which now became known as Westminster Presbyterian church, affiliated to the Presbyterian Church in the United States of America. The Westminster Church, housed in a building both 'handsome and commodious', soon became strong and vigorous, owing largely to the attraction of Watts' preaching and his policy of house-to-house visitation. But the going was often very difficult, especially in the very early years.

Quite apart from his work, a major cause for concern in the experience of the minister at Westminster was the state of Mrs Watts' health, which was adversely affected by the climate in Philadelphia. In 1861 she returned to Ireland to recuperate, but intended making only a short visit. For one thing, she could not contemplate a protracted separation from her husband; and for another, the American states were at that time in the throes of Civil War. Their reunion took place, however, in Ireland as the PCUSA General Assembly appointed Robert Watts their delegate to the General Assembly in Ireland in 1862. In June of that year he was once again on Irish soil, and a resolution was passed by the Irish

Presbyterian Church to the effect 'That the Assembly gladly welcomed amongst them their brother brought up in the bosom of this Church but especially as the trusted delegate of the General Assembly of the Presbyterian Church in America and they cordially reciprocated the fraternal regards conveyed from our brethren'.

The joy associated with this visit to the homeland and the reunion with his family was tempered by news that reached Watts from Philadelphia. The reports suggested that the city was likely to be attacked by the Confederate forces, and already the Westminster Church was being used as a military hospital. Watts returned to his charge immediately but he returned alone. There was much to be done besides the normal round of pastoral duties, especially in connection with those who had been wounded in battle. Watts was indefatigable, and proved once more that he was a pastor devoted to his people.

It became increasingly obvious, however, that the separation from his family could not go on indefinitely, and ultimately Watts came to the conclusion that he must resign from the pastorate at Westminster. This decision was reached only after much prayer and consultation with trusted friends. One of these friends was Dr Chester of the Board of Education, for which body Watts had acted for many years as Secretary. The matter was discussed with his wife by correspondence, and in November 1862 he wrote to her as follows:

> 'I have had several talks lately with Dr Chester. Your health is the only ground which he would hear of as justifying my removal, with such prospects as the Westminster, the Board of Education and the country offer to me and my family'.

In the course of time Watts tendered his resignation to the fellowship at Westminster Church, and the tender regard in which they held their pastor is seen in the fact that the people wept openly when his letter of resignation was read. Resolutions couched in the most loving terms were passed by the church exhibiting the esteem in which the minister was held. After all, out of a spiritual wilderness a strong, vigorous church had been formed largely through the efforts of the one who was now to be removed from them. The concern of the Westminster congregation was reflected in the credentials supplied to Watts by the Presbytery of Philadelphia.

Watts left Philadelphia on Monday, 16th March 1863 and travelled to Boston. From there he sailed on Wednesday, 18th March for Cork and landed at Queenstown on Saturday, 28th March. He had no idea of the way in which Providence would lead him, but his faith and constancy, born of his Reformation theology which bows to the Sovereignty of God in all things, bade him be strong, nothing doubting, until God would make clear the next step.

The Second Pastorate

When Robert Watts landed in Ireland on the 28th March 1863 he had no idea of how or where he would be settled as pastor. He had, of course, had correspondence with Irish ministers, notably Dr Gibson, but this had not provided any concrete arrangements. Watts, however, throughout the period between his resignation from Westminster and his settlement in his second pastorate, expressed the confidence he had that God was in complete control of the situation. Thus he writes,

> '... I can only leave the whole matter to be solved by Him who has guided us thus far. He seeth the end from the beginning. God has His eye on a place for us ...' In another letter he wrote: 'I am relieved and feel free as I am altogether and unreservedly in the Hand of God. The Lord is my shepherd, I shall not want'.

When Watts landed in Ireland and journeyed from Cork to Dublin his train was a few minutes late on arrival and he missed his connection to Belfast. This necessitated his remaining in Dublin over the weekend and frustrated his hopes of reaching his family at Summer Hill by Saturday night. This event, though disadvantageous from one point of view, was fraught with significance, and was ever afterwards regarded by Watts as the workings of providence. On Saturday, 28th March 1863, the very date that Watts once again set foot on Irish soil, the Reverend James Edgar, minister of Lower Gloucester Street Presbyterian Church,

Dublin, died. (Lower Gloucester Street Church is now Clontarf). His illness had been brief and arrangements were speedily put in hand to supply the vacant pulpit. Watts conducted the services there that same weekend, and eventually he was asked to preach as a candidate and was unanimously chosen as Edgar's successor.

The Watts family arrived in Dublin in June and took up residence in the manse in Great Charles' Street which had been built for his predecessor. According to the Church Minutes, 'The Reverend Robert Watts was entertained at a social meeting held in the Rotunda which was attended by members of other congregations'. His first meeting with the Kirk Session was held on the 15th September 1863 and his stipend is recorded at £150 per annum. Meantime, he had been received by the General Assembly in July when his Credentials from the Presbytery of Philadelphia were read.

The experience gained by Watts in his mission work at Moyamensing in Philadelphia made him the ideal choice for such a charge as Lower Gloucester Street. Gibson records that Watts was 'strongly attached to the generous and intellectual people of the metropolis' and, as in Philadelphia, he soon became recognised as an outstanding preacher. He was called upon to preach on such important occasions as the Calvin Tercentenary, when Watts delivered an address in the Metropolitan Hall, Dublin, entitled 'Calvin and Calvinism'. In addition it soon became evident that the new minister of Lower Gloucester Street congregation was 'an accomplished and successful teacher of young men in theological subjects'. May years after Watts' removal from Dublin one of the elders of the Gloucester Street Church proudly showed to Gibson a syllabus of subjects drawn up and taught by Watts to the young men of the city.

The degree of Doctor of Divinity was conferred by Westminster College, Fulton, Missouri in 1864. From that date he is always, in the minutes of the Lower Gloucester Street congregation, referred to as Doctor Watts.

We have noted that the experience gained by him in Philadelphia proved invaluable when he moved to the work in Dublin. There was much to be done, and the new minister shouldered the burden from the outset. Writing to his wife on the subject of the necessity of remaining in Belfast an extra day during a visit to the North, he explained that it was vital to the interests of his new charge. 'The interests of Gloucester Street and its claims as an agency for extending Christ's kingdom in the metropolis should be known at headquarters. If we are to build, we must call upon the church at large to help us and as a preliminary, we must be known'. Writing again to his wife from Belfast he mentions some of his early contacts, among them Dr Edgar, Professor of Theology in the Presbyterian College in that city. Little did he realise that the time would shortly come when Providence would remove Edgar by death and replace him in the Chair of Theology by Watts himself. For, in 1866, Dr Edgar died and Watts was unanimously chosen to succeed him in his professorial capacity. Thus Watts succeeded an Edgar in Dublin and an Edgar in Belfast.

Had the removal of Watts simply been to another congregation, that move would have been opposed by Lower Gloucester Street as the laws of the General Assembly allowed, but their recognition of the importance of the professorial work and their conviction that God had clearly guided in the matter prevented them from pursuing that course. Instead, they honoured their pastor and his family at a congregational meeting when gifts were presented and an address was read. To this Watts fittingly replied. Thus his second pastorate came to an end and Watts was destined to devote himself to teaching the rising generation of ministers, though he never relinquished his right to preach nor lost his love of preaching. He supplied many pulpits during his College life (notably May Street, Belfast) and held himself in readiness at all times to assist his ministerial colleagues in the pulpit. In his reply to the Church's farewell address he says, 'In leaving you I am not surrendering this high office (of an Ambassador of Christ) or changing my estimate of its dignity or importance. But in proportion as I esteem that holy calling I must value every institution which bears upon the raising up, qualifying and sending forth of the heralds of redemption'.

The Influence of Robert Watts on Reformed Witness

'One cannot think of Robert Watts without thinking of Charles Hodge'. So wrote Robert Allen, and his words really lay the foundation for any assessment of the influence exerted by Watts on the Reformed Witness of his day. Another has written: 'Hodge never had a more appreciative pupil nor one who more affectionately cherished the memory of his saintly teacher'. Indeed it is interesting to note that Watts dedicated his book *'The Newer Criticism and the Analogy of the Faith'*, to the memory of three outstanding Calvinist theologians, Hodge among them. The dedication reads: 'To the memory of Dr Thomas Chalmers, Dr William Cunningham and Dr Charles Hodge, this contribution to the defence of the Faith for which they so mightily contended, is affectionately inscribed by the Author'.

Watts was, therefore, very much a theologian of the Princeton School, and it was the Princeton Theology that he wielded so successfully in influencing an entire generation of ministers who trained under him.

In addition, he enjoyed the confidence of some of the greatest Reformed theologians of his day as, for example and in addition to the Hodge family, the justly celebrated Benjamin Breckenridge Warfield. Watts also mentions in his letters Professor W H Green and Professor McCosh, which shows that he was perfectly at home in the wider Princeton context.

But whilst this was the orbit in which Watts moved, it must be emphasised that his reputation as a theologian, preacher, writer and controversialist was not built upon the merits of other men. His reputation stemmed from his own indefatigable labours, so that one could say of him, 'The name of Dr Watts is known and honoured here (America) as it is at home'. Gibson goes somewhat further: 'In Great Britain and in America he was honoured by multitudes for the unflinching opposition he offered to every inroad, from whatever quarter, upon that venerable system of doctrine embodied in our standards'. Nevertheless, one who signed himself simply as 'a brother minister' could write:

'Yet with all his controversies and the strictness of his theological views he combined a kindliness and gentleness which endeared him to many. The austerity of the controversialist was forgotten in the tenderness and geniality of the friend'.

The influence of Watts, however, was not always exerted in controversy. Kirkpatrick seeks to do justice to this when he says:

'Ireland never gave a more worthy man to America than Robert Watts and America repaid the gift with interest when she restored a man so well equipped for the peerless work Dr Watts has done for confessional and Pauline truth in the pulpit, on the platform, through the press and in the distinguished place he held as a teacher of theology and educator of the rising ministry of the Irish Presbyterian Church'.

In these words we have a useful outline which may be employed as the framework for our consideration of this theme. The influence of Watts will therefore be viewed in relation to the pulpit, the platform, the press and the professorial chair.

Watts as a Preacher

The influence of Watts can be seen, first of all, in his preaching, which was always in great demand. His ability in the pulpit was recognised early when, some weeks before the conclusion of his course at Princeton, as we have seen, he was appointed to the very difficult work at Moyamensing. The fact that this mission station became a flourishing church may, in large part, be attributed to his powerful proclamation of the Word. At Westminster he enjoyed, in his preaching, a rapport with his congregation that made him loath to leave them. Writing to his wife, he says: 'When in the Westminster on the Sabbath, with a full house hanging in wrapt attention on the Word of Life, I feel at home'.

This type of experience permitted Watts to describe the Westminster Church as 'a grand theatre for action'. His letters abound with references to his preaching in the Westminster Church and reveal something of his overriding concern for the instruction of his people in the Word of God. Of course, there were attempts to attract him to other churches, notably, perhaps, to the Cooke Church in Toronto, but these overtures met with no success. Writing later to his wife during a visit to Toronto he says:

> 'I preached in the morning in the Cooke Church of which our old friend, Mr Gregg, is Pastor. The Honourable George Brown with whom I dined, reminded me that I was nearly being pastor of that church. You remember that incident in my Philadelphia history when I declined to leave Westminster.'

But what kind of a preacher was Watts? His preaching was scriptural, dogmatic, authoritative, doctrinal, sometimes topical, substantial and always applied with considerable power. The flowery, oratorical and often philosophical manner of preaching which characterised much of the pulpit-work of the 18th and early 19th centuries was gradually giving way to a simpler and much more direct style of address. A greater homiletic element was creeping in to make it easier for the congregation to follow the sermon. Some of the pulpit giants such as C H Spurgeon favoured a threefold division but there is no evidence to suggest that Watts bound himself to any such arrangement. Indeed, quite the reverse is true for there are records of sermons which are divided in a two-, three-, and four-fold manner.

Recognising that the primary task of the preacher is to expound the Word of God, Watts ensured that his sermons were always expository. Nevertheless, the sermon was often built upon a theme as, for example, when he preached on Ephesians 1:6 - 'To the Praise of the Glory of His Grace wherein He hath made us accepted in the Beloved'. The theme was: 'The ultimate design of God in the Economy of Redemption'. Again, when Watts preached from Psalm 45:13 - 'The King's daughter is all-glorious within. Her garments are of wrought gold', his subject was: 'The Glory and Dignity of the Church'.

Watts sometimes preached on themes such as 'Millennarianism' and 'Inspiration' and often he would receive requests to repeat those sermons in other centres. His orations on the former topic gave rise to a series of articles published in the 'Witness', and among the many times he preached on the subject of Inspiration we may mention June 27th 1880. This was, of course, the time of great agitation in various church circles regarding the propagation by W Robertson Smith of the higher critical views of the Graf-Wellhausen School. On this particular occasion Watts had been asked by the Reverend Mr Black of Inverness to preach on the theme of Inspiration. Such was the tremendous interest in the subject that the church building was filled to overflowing, and wherever Watts went in that entire area to speak on the subject he experienced the same overwhelming response to his discourses. In a letter he wrote: 'Yesterday evening was the climax thus far of our meetings. Mr Robertson estimated that there were 2,000 present'. Watts, then, was considered one of the outstanding champions of the orthodox doctrine and the opportunity of hearing him speak was eagerly embraced by thousands.

Though often in the company of men who were distinguished preachers in their own right, Watts was sometimes singled out to preach. This often happened when he was representing the Irish Presbyterian Church at Conventions where the leading figures from the various branches of presbyterianism would be present. Writing to his wife from New York he says, 'We had no service on board on the day we left Queenstown but Doctors Hutcheson, McLeod, Graham and I went to Mr Simpson's church to worship (and) the result was that I was constrained to preach'. Nevertheless, Watts could appreciate the preaching of others. In the letter quoted, he goes on to say, 'On Sabbath we had a sermon which was a sermon indeed from Dr Main'. He, in another letter, describes the preaching of Dr Sprague, the American theologian who gave the main address at the Semi-centenary of the opening of Princeton Seminary. 'It was just magnificent', says Watts. 'He left nothing unsaid that ought to have been said, and said nothing that should not have had a place on the occasion'. At another time he writes: 'We went into the church and heard Dr Hamilton of London. I have never listened to so great a treat'. Further tributes were paid to other preachers as, for example, to Doctors Horatio Bonar and MacKay. 'Dr H. Bonar who was at the Assembly, spoke on the "Ark of the Covenant" very beautifully. Dr MacKay of Hull, author of

"Grace and Truth", spoke on the Glory between the Cherubim in a very clever and stirring style'. We need, however, to compare this with his attitude to a Free Church preacher who took as his text Ecclesiastes 3:15 and whose 'doctrine was that whilst sin may be pardoned even the grace of God and the blood of Christ are helpless to do away with its effects ... Peter will be known in heaven by the traces of his blasphemy and denial and Paul will be known by the traces left by his course of persecution. Eternity itself will not be able to remove the effects of the sins committed even by these eminent servants of God'. Watts goes on to describe his own reaction: 'I could hardly keep my seat. I reached over to the Chairman and taking his large Bible, I pointed out to him (the Chairman) Ephesians 5:27, "that He might present it to Himself a glorious church not having spot or wrinkle or any such thing but that it should be holy and without blemish". And when the preacher sat down beside me I asked him did he believe that the Gospel reached only the *reatus* (guilt) of sins and did not reach the *macula* (stain, pollution)'. The preacher apologised for producing what he called a wrong impression.

Watts also preached for some of the really outstanding ministers of his day. He occupied, on several occasions, the pulpit of the brilliant, if somewhat eccentric, Robert Smith Candlish of Free St George's Church, Edinburgh. In a letter to his wife he notes that he had been 'asked by Dr Candlish's special request to preach in his church'.

Among the many other special occasions when Watts was the preacher we may mention the Lutherfest in Wittenberg, Germany, when he says, 'I spoke as freely in the German as I ever did in my own mother tongue'; and at the opening session of the World Presbyterian Alliance held in Belfast in 1884. It is worth noting, in passing, that when the World Presbyterian Alliance held its International Convention in Belfast, the entire organisation devolved upon Robert Watts. He had been appointed co-Chairman with the venerable Dr Knox, a widely respected founder-member of the Alliance. Knox died soon after and Watts was left to organise the entire event. His efforts were acknowledged by the convention, which included such outstanding theologians as B B Warfield, A A Hodge and W G T Shedd.

It is one thing, however, to be an outstanding preacher on a particular occasion and quite another to maintain a consistently high ministry in the local pastoral context. It is therefore of importance to note the estimate of Watts' preaching entertained by the two congregations he served in a pastoral capacity. We have noted already how Watts described his congregation at Westminster as 'hanging with wrapt attention on the Word of Life', and when he removed from Philadelphia to Dublin, his former charge sought to recall him. One minister wrote of him:

> 'Watts lived in the affections of older people strongly who never tired in relating interesting incidents in his ministry. His removal to Ireland broke their hearts for they felt they might never see his like again. They sought to recall him from Dublin but in vain'.

As far as the Dublin congregation was concerned, among the other excellences noted in their farewell to the pastor, his preaching was singled out for special mention.

> 'We will not attempt to describe our sense of the faithfulness and ability with which you have discharged your ministerial duties during the period of three years and some months that you have been in charge of this congregation, the pleasure and profit we have derived from your discourses in the pulpit...'.

Other churches thought the same. During his professoriate, for example, Watts served the May Street Presbyterian Church during a one-year interregnum. When the time came for the church to bid him farewell they presented Watts and his wife with handsome gifts, and once again his preaching was particularly mentioned. We see, then, that the opinion of his two settled congregations coincided with the estimates of those congregations to which he preached either in an interim or visiting capacity.

It is a striking fact that Watts was evidently fond of preaching from the book of Revelation. This is particularly interesting because the Belfast Professor subscribed to the historico-grammatical hermeneutic so successfully employed by John Calvin. This hermeneutic is, however, particularly difficult to apply to a highly symbolical book like the Apocalypse and we recall that the great reformer published no commentary on it, saying simply that he did not understand it. Yet Watts turned to it again and again for his texts. Preaching at the opening session of the World Presbyterian Alliance held in Belfast in 1884, Watts took as his text Revelation 5:6, 7. Yet his opening remarks placed the text firmly in its historical context by showing that it was a continuation of the narrative in Acts 1:9-11 where we have the record of the ascension of Jesus Christ.

The Professor evidently believed in 'centralising the pulpit' and he always took his full measure of time. Allen records that Watts 'preached with great acceptance in many pulpits' but then adds a little unkindly, 'though at great length'. When Watts preached in the May Street Church on the subject of 'Millennarianism' the address lasted for an hour and a half during which time 'interest never flagged for a moment'. On another occasion the sermon lasted for one and three quarter hours and in a letter to his daughter in which he describes another service he records (with a trace of self-reproach) 'I spoke only an hour'. Indeed, after he had preached to Mr Black's congregation to which we have already referred, he recorded that 'the audience would have listened much longer had I continued to speak'.

Though it is evident that the sermons of Robert Watts were the result of patient and painstaking study, they were delivered without recourse to manuscript or notes of any kind. When he visited Lafayette College (where he had studied in 1848) he was invited to preach the Baccalaureate sermon for the Brainerd Society. Later, the President of the College, Dr Cattell, asked for notes of the sermon. As no manuscript had been used Watts had to spend a considerable part of the following day writing notes to satisfy the request of the President.

The entire emphasis of the preaching of Robert Watts, however, was made to fall upon the exposition of the Word of God. Sometimes thematic, always expository and presented in language at once the most chaste and apposite, the sermons of Watts provided spiritual nourishment for those who flocked to hear him. Thus we see that the opinions of eminent judges, so laudatory of Watts' ability as a preacher, were not in any way exaggerations. One minister wrote of him:

> 'For many years Dr Watts was unwearying in occupying the pulpits of his brethren. His sermons were unique in their character, being built up of massive reasoning founded on the fundamental truths of the Calvinistic system. The cogency of his subject was often illuminated by the most intense fervour and always relieved by a rich vein of tenderness and sympathy'.

Another recorded his assessment of Watts thus:

> 'Dr Watts was no ordinary theologian as he was no ordinary minister. His work was not confined to his Chair. He was always ready to officiate for his brethren throughout the Church and was thus a means of stimulating and encouraging many of their congregations. He was an orthodox theologian but he was of the Spurgeon type. None in preaching gave a freer or more urgent offer of salvation to the sinner'.

It is no wonder then that the Presbytery of Philadelphia, in dissolving the pastoral relationship between Watts and Westminster Church, should have written: 'We add our united testimony to that of his church in respect to the character and life of our esteemed brother. We honour him as a sound and learned expositor of Scripture, an instructive and eloquent preacher ...'. Said another of Watts: 'He had devoted his life to the vindication of those great truths of Scripture which have been assailed and which, by his life, he adorned'.

The Professoriate

When, in 1866, Dr Edgar died, it was necessary for a special General Assembly to be convened for the purpose of appointing his successor in the Chair of Theology at the Presbyterian College, Belfast. There was a very large attendance at that special Assembly when ministers and elders from all parts of Ireland met to deal with this most important matter under the moderatorship of the Rev. Dr Wilson of Limerick. Edgar had been Professor of Theology jointly with Rev. Samuel Hanna from 1840 - the date of the Union between the Irish Presbyterian Synod of Ulster and the Secession Church. He became sole Professor of Theology when Hanna died in 1852 and held the post until his own death in 1866.

There were some delegates who thought that the matter should be postponed until the regular Assembly would meet during the following June but the Amendment to that effect was defeated by 187 votes. There was, in fact, only one nomination for the vacancy - Dr Watts - who had been induced by a largely-signed petition to offer himself for the Chair. He was proposed by the Rev. Dr James Morgan of Fisherwick Place Church, Belfast and seconded by the Rev. (later Professor) Henry Wallace and they were permitted to address the Assembly on the merits of the candidate.

The appointment was approved by the unanimous vote of the Assembly and 'Dr Watts, amid the warmest demonstrations of enthusiasm, ascended the platform and signed the usual formula of subscription to the Westminster Confession of Faith.' The unanimity that prevailed was a matter of thanksgiving to all concerned but to none more than to Morgan and Wallace. An extract from the diary of the former will show with what fear and trepidation he had anticipated that special Assembly.

'October 6th - I have much cause to bless the Lord for His great goodness in the settlement of our Theological Chair. Dr Watts has been chosen to it by the unanimous voice of the Assembly. It pleased the Lord to employ me as an unworthy advocate for His servant. I had been asked to nominate him and consented. On the evening before the day of the election all necessary documents - degree, diploma, testimonials etc from the United States, were brought to me. These had only arrived (at least, some of the most important of them) the day before. I got an hour to examine and arrange them. They were very satisfactory and the Lord directed me in using them. I entered on the duty with fear and trembling and was very doubtful of the issue. The Lord stood by me and my statement was most favourably received. I was followed by my beloved friend and brother, Henry Wallace, who delivered an excellent address. All opposition was disarmed. None spoke against our motion. The election was unanimous. It has given unbounded satisfaction in the town and everywhere. Lord, be Thou exalted! And oh! do Thou bless and prepare Thy servant for his great work.'

That the confidence reposed in Watts that day by his Church was not misplaced, his subsequent work as professor abundantly demonstrated. His own experience of six years in American Colleges of Higher Learning had given him a very high estimate of a tutor's responsibilities and his career testifies eloquently to the fact that he enjoyed a large measure of success in achieving those standards himself.

Because of the exceptionally short time between his election to the Chair and the opening of the College session a great deal of heavy preparatory work had to be undertaken immediately. This severely overtaxed his strength and there was some apprehension with regard to his future health. However, at the end of Watts' first year as Professor of Theology, Dr Morgan could record, 'Dr Watts has ended his first session as successor to Dr Edgar, with the highest approval'.

Certainly Watts was much the superior man for the Chair of Systematic Theology. Edgar has been described as 'a man of great mental power and burning zeal'. Of course, Watts enjoyed those characteristics too but the difference between them lay in the approach to the work in the classroom. 'As a Professor', writes Edgar's biographer, 'he had no taste for the minute dissection of theological systems and he did not care to enter into the subtleties of mental analysis. In lecturing, as in other matters, he was guided very much by impulse, and he accordingly took up topics in his class, not in the order of their logical arrangement, but as they happened to make an impression on his own ardent mind'. Watts, on the other hand, was very much the systematic theologian with immense logical powers. Indeed, his logic has been described as 'relentless'. The acumen and skill with which he exposed the weaknesses in other systems of theology made him respected even by those who held no particular love for him. Marcus Dods the Younger, who turned his back upon the evangelical faith of his father and his Church, and who in other places wrote in the most scathing terms about Watts, was nevertheless constrained to write, 'Grant him his premises and his conclusions inevitably follow'.

Watts enjoyed the esteem and confidence of his students who regarded him as the most interesting lecturer in the College. Indeed, he was closer to the students than any of the other professors by virtue of the fact that he was Secretary of the College and of the Students' Chambers. This brought him into very close contact with the social and domestic aspects of student life from the time he assumed these extra responsibilities (1878) until his death in 1895. His successor, Rev Professor Hamill, said 'He was ... a wise and kindly counsellor when they sought his advice; a true, staunch friend whose friendliness none of us every appealed to in vain'.

Each Tuesday during the session, four or five students would visit his study in turn and preach a sermon or deliver a lecture on a pre-arranged text or theme. The discourses were then subjected to kindly but firm criticism by Watts, and many an aspiring preacher had reason to be thankful for his guidance in matters concerning homiletics. The students approached these sessions with fear and trembling but were speedily put at ease by one who knew their difficulties and sought only to help. These homiletics classes lasted from 4 pm until 9 pm.

In his history of the College, Allen has a chapter entitled 'A Citadel of Calvinism', and there can be no doubt whatever that this was the direct result of the powerful advocacy of that system in the College by Watts. Allen says: 'He was a bulwark of orthodoxy' but then adds without justification, 'and more Calvinistic than Calvin himself'. What is certain, however, is that Watts sought to make the College an institution based on the Princeton model and there is ample evidence to justify the remark that Assembly's College became 'the recognised headquarters of Calvinism' and 'a Second Princeton'.

Indeed, it was this recognition of the Reformed stance adopted by the College, and in particular of Watts' contribution in that direction, that attracted to Belfast many theological students from other countries. This is particularly the case with regard to

Scotland, and it is noted that, at one time, there were as many as seven Scottish students who had come to Belfast to sit at the feet of Watts but who, nevertheless, according to their traditions, stood for prayer and sat silent during the singing of hymns. Among them were John MacLeod, George MacKay and Donald Beaton.

Watts was generally regarded as the most outstanding representative of the Princeton Theology in the British Isles, and it is a matter of record that during Watts' tenure of office the College enjoyed a worldwide reputation for scholarship and orthodoxy. It is a melancholy thought that 'his death marked the end of an era in the College'. So highly did the Free Presbyterian Church of Scotland regard Watts that, immediately after he died, its Synod passed a motion that no further students should be sent to train at the Presbyterian College, Belfast.

Professor Robert Watts, then, was the man 'who did most to give the College a reputation for virile Calvinism', who 'inspired others to learn', in whose presence 'theology was more exciting than it is wont to be' and who could 'make the dry bones of theology as marrow and fatness'. We need not wonder, then, that other institutions sought to attract him and to secure his services. In 1876 the Chair of Apologetics and Exegesis of the Gospels fell vacant at Aberdeen and Watts was proposed by several presbyteries of the Free Church of Scotland. He, however, wrote immediately declining to be considered as a candidate. In 1878 he declined the office of Principal and Primarius Professor of Theology at Melbourne, Australia. He had been designated by a Commission composed of representatives from the Church of Scotland, the Free Church of Scotland and the Presbyterian Church in Ireland. The selection had been entrusted to the Rev. Principal Robert Rainy, Professor Robert Flint and Professor J L Porter.

In 1881, though he was not a candidate, Watts was nominated by several Synods and Presbyteries for the Chair of Systematic Theology at New College, Edinburgh. He was defeated by 364 votes to 200 and there can be no doubt that one of the main reasons for his rejection was his advocacy of instrumental music in the public worship of God. The Free Church of Scotland does not approve the use of instrumental music and Watts' well-known advocacy of the opposite position was successfully urged against him.

In the midst of the pressures associated with these various 'calls' to professorial chairs, Watts served his church as Moderator in 1879. He approached his work as Moderator in the same dedicated manner as he did his work as Professor and certainly dignified the office to which he had been called. His humour was in evidence at the General Assembly when he was Moderator. One speaker referred to another as 'a silly ass'. The offended party asked the Moderator if the offender was allowed to call him a silly ass. 'Certainly,' replied Watts, 'as long as he calls you brother!'

That Watts commanded the respect and confidence of various denominations within Presbyterianism and that he was either nominated or selected for various important professorial appointments without candidature speaks eloquently of the influence he exerted upon the church of his time. His successor in the Chair of Systematic Theology in Belfast, Professor Hamill, in his inaugural address, paid tribute to Watts' influence in these words:

> 'Far beyond the classroom his influence and fame travelled where the living voice did not reach. Volume after volume from his pen, dealing with the multiform phases of the controversies between scientific speculation and evangelical theology, made him known as among the ablest defenders of the faith which was once for all delivered unto the saints.'

In the opinion of many he was 'the most distinguished theologian that the Irish Presbyterian Church ever produced'.

One minister wrote of him: 'Dr Watts was a very strong Calvinist and it is questionable if any theologian had ever a firmer grasp of the principles of that system of theology. He was quick to detect the weak points, philosophical and theological, in other systems and equally quick to defend what he regarded as the orthodox position'.

In the same place, Rev. Dr Williamson's remarks are recorded. On the Sabbath after Watts' death the minister of Fisherwick said:

'I think I speak advisedly and with the full understanding of what I say when I affirm that he has not left behind him in all our borders one so fully acquainted in the Reformation doctrines and so able to assert and maintain them.'

On the Platform and in the Press

Robert Watts was a force to be reckoned with when he mounted a platform to speak on behalf of historic Christianity and to defend the faith once delivered to the saints. Some of the ablest men in their respective spheres evidently recognised this and it was, perhaps, an indication of their shrewdness that they refused to meet him in public debate. Writes one minister:

'The sensation created by Dr Tyndall's address at the meeting of the British Association in Belfast in 1874 will be remembered by many and the prompt and able reply of Dr Watts, supplemented by his giving to Professor Tyndall a challenge to a public discussion of his subject, which was declined.'

We have referred to the meetings in Belfast of the British Association. The year was 1874. Knowing that the theory of evolution would find expression there, Watts wrote asking to be permitted to deliver a paper at one of the sessions. His request was declined. He then secured the Elmwood Church for lunchtime services during which he delivered addresses against the evolutionary theory. The building was packed to capacity and the addresses later published. In addition, as we have seen, Watts offered to meet the chief evolutionary spokesman, Dr Tyndall, in public debate, but this, too, was declined. But whether his opponents would meet him or not, Watts delivered addresses and lectures in which the public at large was presented with a Christian apologetic which was second to none.

The main burden of his public lectures was three-fold. He was much concerned with the twin doctrines of Revelation and Inspiration, and time and again he returned to an elucidation of these themes. Allied to that, he was the stern opponent of every form of rationalism and he lifted up the banner against the novel ideas and higher critical tendencies which had reared their heads in the church of his day. Thirdly, he was concerned to expose the fallacious arguments and gratuitous assumptions of the evolutionary hypothesis.

Whilst Watts was in continual demand as a lecturer on all these themes, his platform work in connection with the exposure of the barrenness of rationalism was most marked during the W Robertson Smith controversy. During the latter half of the decade 1870-1880, therefore, Watts made repeated visits to Scotland to present the case for Reformed orthodoxy.

On the 22nd September 1878 the Kinnaird Hall, Dundee, was crowded to capacity to hear Watts. Describing the scene in a letter he writes:

> 'The Kinnaird Hall was filled in every part; balconies, gallery and orchestra. The Scotch pay very particular attention just now as they are heart-sick and wearied out with broad churchism. From all that I can learn there is a great reaction setting in against latitudinarian views which have been so long current in the Establishment and which have had some countenance even in the Free Church.'

To his daughter he writes about a meeting in Dundee where '... the entrance to the hall was blocked with an ever-increasing crowd. On consultation we adjoined to a neighbouring church but, as it was in the hall so was it in the church. A fresh consultation held and a fresh adjournment was made to the Kinnaird Hall. As soon as the decision was announced the people made a headlong rush for the new centre of gathering and found the place already nearly filled with those who had been outside the church. We got in by a side door ... The body of the hall was not only packed but also the orchestra and the platform.'

Invited to lecture in Perth by the Rev. Mr Gibson, Watts describes the occasion in the following words: 'My lecture in Perth on Herbert Spencer's Biological Hypothesis came off very well. There were many ministers present and a large audience and intelligent attention given for an hour and three quarters. Mr Gibson was very pleased'.

Watts sometimes notes the reaction of the ministers present, evidently feeling the importance of influencing them for the truth. 'The ministers here have been exceedingly kind to me and greatly pleased ...'. 'All the ministers are very kind and tell me that my work will do great good'. 'There were several ministers present who thanked me for the service I had rendered to the cause of Truth'.

These Scottish tours were extremely arduous, and often in the midst of the planned itinerary Watts was requested to deliver additional lectures. Thus he could write: 'Yesterday evening was the climax thus far of our meetings. I am asked to lecture in Edinburgh and will leave for that city on Wednesday'.

The Belfast Professor was utterly unafraid when it came to defending orthodoxy against any form of deviation whatever. Nor was he reticent about taking part in the debates in the General Assembly and World Presbyterian Alliance. His contributions to the debates in the Alliance were often regarded as 'the last word' and it is interesting to note the comment of an Irish Presbyterian minister as he recalls a scene in the General Assembly. 'When a debate was provoked in our Assembly on the question of Believers' Assurance, Dr Watts' expositions of the conflicting views of that question were received by the crowded house as exhaustive of the subject'.

The diligence of Watts in the propagation of Truth was not confined to pulpit, platform and professorial work. It was also abundantly evident in his contributions to the religious press. Says Allen:

> 'It was as a champion of Calvinistic orthodoxy, waging an unceasing warfare against every form of progressive theological thought that he is chiefly to be remembered. This he did in his lectures, in his books, in periodicals and in the press.'

Even a cursory glance at the Historical Introduction to Watts' Writings, contained in the present writer's doctoral thesis, should be sufficient to enable the candid reader to endorse Allen's remark that 'the bare enumeration of his published works indicates how widely he had roamed in the world of theology and philosophy'. Another has written in similar vein: 'The Professor had made the whole field of Biblical Theology his own and was prepared to defend it against all impugners'.

In the bibliography to my doctoral thesis I have noted sixteen titles by Watts, though many lengthy articles appear as fugitive pieces in such journals as *'The British and Foreign Evangelical Review'*, *'The Witness'* and *'Princeton Review'*. However, Watts' 'magnum opus' is, undoubtedly, *'The Rule of Faith and the Doctrine of Inspiration'*, the published version of the Carey Lectures of 1884 and coming off the press in 1885. This is a masterly defence of the orthodox doctrine of the Inspiration of the Holy Scriptures and has been described by Professor H D MacDonald as 'one of the strongest statements of the traditional view of Inspiration'.

Other very successful books included *'The New Apologetic and its Claims to Scriptural Authority'* and *'The Newer Criticism and the Analogy of Faith'*. This latter volume was his reply to the lectures of W Robertson Smith on the Old Testament and the Jewish Church. In addition, besides writing such books as 'The Reign of Causality' and 'Essays Theological and Scientific', he was one of the learned contributors to a highly-prized volume entitled 'Lex Mosaica'. His published works won the highest praise and approbation in such influential journals and papers as 'New York Observer', 'The Presbyterian Churchman', 'The English Churchman', 'Sword and Trowel' and 'Christian World Pulpit'. His tracts and pamphlets were widely distributed and carried his teachings to multitudes who could not be reached through the spoken word. Charles Haddon Spurgeon wrote of *The New Apologetic*: 'As able as it is sound and as scriptural as it is logical'.

This is not to say that the published works of Watts met with universal acclaim. As Allen says, 'The critic invites criticism'; and the one who, with meticulous care, scrutinised, evaluated and criticised the works of such theologians as A M Fairbairn, Bruce and Dods became, on occasion, the target of their attacks. Marcus Dods regarded Watts as 'one of those unhappily constituted men who cannot write unless they are angry'. He was, in Dods' opinion 'a clever logician, deftly manipulating theological formulae, but whether these have any relation to reality he never inquires. He is essentially an advocate, not a judge. He belongs, craving Horace's pardon, to the *irritabile genus disputatorum*'. The editor of The Expositor, in whose pages these criticisms appeared, refused to publish Watts' reply wherein he clearly demonstrated the folly of Dods. Wrote Watts:

> 'If these formulae then are doctrinal unrealities, it must follow that in condemning me for defending them he is simply condemning himself for subscribing them. I have simply been doing what he bound himself to do both by his ordination and his installation vows.'

Allen continues:

> 'Watts then went on to apply to the new Scottish school the words used by Claus Harms of the German rationalists of his day: "It is a singular pretension to demand liberty to teach a new faith from the seat of a chair which the old faith established and by a mouth which the old faith feeds."'

Watts' critique of Robertson Smith invoked the wrath of *The Scotsman* which referred to the Belfast Professor's 324 page book as 'an overgrown pamphlet'. But though they disagreed with him on many points the opponents of Watts were obliged to take cognizance of him because what he wrote carried tremendous influence in many quarters.

One writer remarks: 'His writings ... were in some measure successful in arresting tendencies which he combated with confident vivacity'. The same writer, who can scarcely be accused of enthusiasm for Watts, further describes him as 'a keen theologian of very conservative views who opposed the tendency of much modern criticism, especially the influence of German exegesis. He studied current speculations with some care in a spirit of uncompromising antagonism'.

This, then, was the man who, for nearly thirty years, 'held at bay with dogged perseverance, the new ideas in theology and Biblical criticism' and there can be absolutely no doubt as to the correctness of the remark made by one of his friends after the death of Watts: 'He has left his mark unmistakably on the age in which he lived'. He was a Mr-Valiant-for-Truth, an able expositor of the Word of God, a preacher of outstanding ability, a compelling author of doctrinal works that instructed the Christian world, a keen controversialist, a vigorous and relentless logician, a wise counsellor and a friend upon whom one could truly rely. He was a pulpiteer, a pamphleteer and a professor but above all, he was a man of God, a workman who needed not to be ashamed, rightly dividing the Word of Truth.

'Soli Deo Gloria'.